BREAKING THROUGH
THE BARRIERS OF *Prayer*

Breaking Through The Barriers of *Prayer*

By
Donna Ringgold

XULON PRESS

Xulon Press
2301 Lucien Way #415
Maitland, FL 32751
407.339.4217
www.xulonpress.com

© 2022 by DONNA RINGGOLD

All rights reserved solely by the author. The author guarantees all contents are original and do not infringe upon the legal rights of any other person or work. No part of this book may be reproduced in any form without the permission of the author.

Due to the changing nature of the Internet, if there are any web addresses, links, or URLs included in this manuscript, these may have been altered and may no longer be accessible. The views and opinions shared in this book belong solely to the author and do not necessarily reflect those of the publisher. The publisher therefore disclaims responsibility for the views or opinions expressed within the work.

Unless otherwise indicated, Scripture quotations taken from the King James Version (KJV)–*public domain.*

Scripture quotations taken from the Holy Bible, New International Version (NIV). Copyright © 1973, 1978, 1984, 2011 by Biblica, Inc.™. Used by permission. All rights reserved.

Scripture quotations taken from the Amplified Bible (AMP). Copyright © 1954, 1958, 1962, 1964, 1965, 1987 by The Lockman Foundation. Used by permission. All rights reserved.

Paperback ISBN-13: 978-1-66285-304-3
Ebook ISBN-13: 978-1-66285-305-0

TABLE OF CONTENTS

Dedication ix
Introduction xi

~~~~~~~~~~~~~~~~~~~~~

Chapter One
GETTING BEYOND YOUR FEAR OF
    PRAYING IN PUBLIC. 1

Chapter Two
ADDRESSING YOUR ATTITUDE
    TOWARD PRAYER 11

Chapter Three
THE PRINCIPLES OF PRAYER 19

Chapter Four
THE WORK OF THE HOLY SPIRIT 31

Chapter Five
THE WORK OF THE HOLY SPIRIT PT. 2 41

Chapter Six
YOUR JOURNEY OF PRAYER 49

Chapter Seven
MAKING A COMMITMENT TO PRAY. 59

EPILOGUE 67

Dedication

This book is dedicated to my three adult children, John, Jacob, and Jerusha. And this book is also committed to my husband, Senior Pastor of Bethel Church. He untiringly pushed, prodded, and believed in me without measure. If it had not been for my family, I probably wouldn't be writing this book right now. I'm grateful to God for processing, developing, and grooming me through it all.

This book is also dedicated to the Women of God who have surrounded me with their prayers, love, support, and acceptance. Their fellowship is unquestionable, significant, and meaningful in my life. And this book is devoted to every sincere believer who wishes to enhance their ability to pray effectively.

INTRODUCTION

This book is an invitation to serious believers who hunger and desire to be more effective in their prayer life. It is an invitation to learn the basic principles of prayer. So, let's turn on our spiritual GPS; (GPS — a physical portable electronic map, a tool to help us find our way in a foreign area; or in a place we've never been before), our iPhone, our Samsung, and or our Android.

Begin to program your attention to 101 Prayer Avenue, in building Luke; Unit 18:1. It is the avenue many new believers are getting familiar with. Yet, those who have been believers for some time have forgotten that such an avenue exists. In this particular building, a class is taught on persevering prayer. A judge gives a widow what she is asking for because her reputation of not giving up and not giving in precedes her.

We are so consumed with the business of life that we don't put a high priority on the things of God. We have turned our attention to our tribulations, persecutions, the cares of this world, and the deceitfulness of riches. (Mark 4:17-19) We have so much pulling at us today that captures our attention away from our first love. (Revelation 2:4) Our ears have become dull of hearing. (Matthew 13:15)

This book is written to introduce to some, and reaffirm to others, how to pray more effectively. What is Prayer? How do we even begin to put our thoughts about our Father in heaven in motion? How do we articulate our prayers to get answers? Do we have to be educated or on a certain level before we can begin the process of learning how to pray? Can we be at home alone, or do we have to be at church to pray? Who do we pray to? Do we pray to Jesus, or do we pray to our heavenly Father? How do we pray for someone sick or in another state or country?

These are some of the questions that we will address in this book. We want you to have a clear understanding of how to pray and how to pray specifically with precision and effectively with results.

This book is a call to obedience! A call to every believer who will hear the Spirit of the Lord calling them to pray. The Word of God says, "men ought to always pray, and faint not." (Luke 18:1) And to "pray without ceasing." (1 Thessalonians 5:17). We are to "pray for one another." (James 5:16). We are told to be, "praying always with all prayer and supplication in the Spirit..." (Ephesians 6:18) We are told to be "…. instant in prayer." (Romans 12:12) So, our Christian lifestyle shouldn't be a calculated missing-in-action behavior, but a habit of enveloped prayer.

Breaking Through the Barriers of Prayer is a book about the numerous times I believe the Holy Spirit wants to commune with us, to give us inspiration on

INTRODUCTION

matters of concern in our hearts. However, some hurdles and roadblocks impede our progress. I have heard countless times from believers about their sleepless nights of tossing and turning, trying to get to sleep. Or maybe even sleeping only three hours, then "bam," lying in bed, eyes wide open. On multiple occasions, some believers would reveal that they would turn on the TV to get back to sleep, clean up the house, or do some reading until they fell back to sleep. In my experience over the years, I have found that in the stillness of the night is when God speaks to me. Now it may not happen with you that particular way, but in many instances, it will.

There was a season in my life when I would keep a journal and pen next to my pillow to be ready when the Holy Spirit would awaken me. I was prepared to write what the Spirit of the Lord was saying to me in the dark. It was challenging the next morning to figure out what I had scribbled in my notebook. Still, God's message and Word were very clear about what He was saying to me in the early hours of the morning.

To break through the barriers, we must recognize the hurdles and roadblocks set in place as a deterrent. Breaking through anything is going to take some determination and conviction. Breaking through the barriers of prayer for me is written in this book. In many ways, I had to overcome a lot of the training and traditions set in stone, so to speak, before I could break through. One primary area was the barriers within myself. Then, I had to overcome the religious rails of tradition in the Baptist Faith.

We intend to focus on the pillars and building blocks of prayer. It encourages believers to be confident and strong in their prayer life.

A barrier is anything built to bar passage, such as a fence or railing. It becomes challenging to break through walls or strongholds because they have always existed. And it is exciting, to say the least, to break out of your box, to create new and fresh ideas. Know this; if God is indeed leading you, those Jericho walls are coming down.

CHAPTER ONE

GETTING BEYOND YOUR FEAR OF PRAYING IN PUBLIC

It may really surprise you at the percentage of people (believers) who are really afraid to pray in a public setting. And you may be one of them. How do I know? Because I was one of them. At a meeting, I would whisper to myself, "I hope they don't ask me to pray. Or maybe I'll just stay out of the room until I know they are finished praying." You find yourself comparing yourself with others who have just prayed.

It was once said that "the thing that you are most afraid of is the thing that the devil is trying to keep you from doing". "In other words, the devil tries his hardest to keep you ignorant in a specific area, and that's the area where you should press in!

Maybe the devil is trying to keep you from going to church regularly because the devil knows that the Word of God is changing and shifting your behavior. The devil knows you are learning to live a holy and sanctified life. <u>Pay attention to the specific attacks</u>

<u>that come in your life.</u> You will get a clue from the episodes about the area that may be your ministry in years to come. Maybe the devil is trying to deceive you into thinking that you just have so many things on your schedule that you can't possibly schedule some prayer time.

Don't ever forget that the devil's job is to kill, steal, and destroy! Go figure! He wants you to be so busy doing everything else you don't have time to pray.

You know the setting, at Wednesday night denominational prayer meeting. The Deacons sing a hymn, read a scripture, and then pray. After which, another hymn is sung, and the floor is opened to anyone who wants to testify, sing a song, or pray. Or it may be at the beginning of a ministry, and you open with prayer.

Well, I was always that person that would say to myself, "Sister Cantaloupe can really pray but not me"! And Brother Watermelon would pray the same prayer every Wednesday night at prayer meetings. If the opportunity ever came to me; all I could think of was, "Lord, thank you for this day; Lord bless me, bless my husband, and bless my children! In Jesus' Name Amen." That would be all of five seconds, and I was through. How could I compare to Sister Cantaloupe, who got up to pray every Wednesday night, and Brother Watermelon, who would follow his memorized prayer behind her?

One of the things that plagued me in my mind was the revisiting of a book on public speaking, which I had read several years ago. I remember vividly reading a statement, "when you open up your mouth to speak, those that hear will know exactly what you are thinking." That one statement kept me from praying out loud in public settings for years. That spirit of fear gripped my spirit and said, "you better not pray. You don't know how to pray, and you call yourself a First Lady, you will sound like a fool, and everyone will know it."

I now know; what I didn't know then was a demon whispering in my ear to keep me from my God-driven purpose. Part of that purpose was to pray, to be an intercessor, to do spiritual warfare, to teach women to pray, and to encourage women not to be afraid. The devil was lying, deceiving, and blocking all God had for me. The devil was blocking me, just with the spirit of fear. Unknowingly, I allowed that fear to control my passion, drive, and desire to pray. I had no idea that God was calling me to the ministry of prayer. And that was the thing I was most afraid of.

My husband, the Senior Pastor, once stated, "the very thing, the greatest fear you have, is the one thing that can never happen to you." Why? Because the devil is lying to you. My attention wasn't on how My Father wanted me to pray but on what other people thought about me when I prayed. That thought, right there, can get you into a lot of trouble. I was afraid of sounding foolish in front of people. I was scared of messing up my words. I was afraid of being vulnerable. I was scared of people judging me. I was afraid!

When you really get a revelation of the scripture in 2 Timothy 1:7 (NIV), it changes your perspective. God doesn't give us a timid spirit. The Spirit God gave us does not make us fearful but gives us power, love, and self-discipline. That didn't even cross my mind. The spirit of fear had gripped and seized my mind. That fear hindered me from seeing anything else! It was an invisible prison that I allowed myself to be locked up in. Thank God for deliverance!

Prayer is one of the most Powerful Weapons. We, as believers, must fight against the enemy! When the spirit of fear is operating in your life, God is put on the back burner, and He is waiting for you to deal with this spirit and walk in victory! The spirit of fear was a hurdle that I needed to break through. Romans 8:15 (NIV) states: "The Spirit you received does not make you slaves so that you live in fear again; rather, the Spirit you received brought about your adoption to sonship." If the spirit of fear is operating in your life, you are functioning as a slave. And a slave is not free. This scripture wasn't even on my radar. One thing is for sure, you can't do it in your own strength. The precious Holy Spirit will lead and help you defeat that spirit of fear that is controlling and manipulating your actions.

God is calling his people to prayer! You must literally hear the call going out into the airwaves. To listen not only to the physical, verbal call, but your spiritual antennas must also be alert to the inner call of the Spirit of God from within for more intimacy with our Father.

When the call goes forth and reaches our spirit and innermost hidden thoughts, a decision, a choice, then begins to enter and work its way through our thought patterns. We may say, "I'm hearing this call in my spirit, but at the same time, I am trying to fit this call into my tight schedule." Many times, the call gets silenced and arm wrestled into the background because we have been taught that the physical or the flesh is more important than the spiritual. This kind of spirit has caused numerous casualties and drove us to miss the move of God in our lives repeatedly. This workaholic, or this busybody spirit, is a spirit that needs to be put in its place. And that place is not ahead of God!

God is so loving and patient with us that He gently calls us in another way to confirm to you and me that *"It's Me Again, trying to get your attention."* It may be that you wake up in the middle of the night at the same time every night. He's gently trying to get your attention.

Have you ever experienced God dealing with you in a specific area of spiritual growth, and nobody but you and God knows what it is? God's Spirit in you begins to jump and leap, confirming what He already has spoken to you. Then there comes a scheduled meeting, an appointment, a setting of gathered people, and a person begins to speak. Right at that moment, you know God is calling and confirming His spoken Word to you. Right at that moment, you might even chuckle and say, "I hear you, Father." Or you may say to yourself, "My Father has a sense of humor."

You may ask yourself, will this call go away? The answer is no! Sometimes it is muffled and gauged because of our unwillingness to allow God to lead and guide our lives. Sometimes it is hindered from coming forth because of the lifestyle we have chosen to live. Sometimes the call is quenched because our priorities are in the wrong order. Sometimes the call gets derailed because we want the glory that belongs only to God. Sometimes the call gets hijacked and given another name because it wants a title; (Apostle, Pastor, Prophet, Evangelist, Teacher, Bishop, Overseer).

Sometimes the call is full of pride and arrogance that it can't possibly be calling them to do something as small as going to pray consistently and regularly. Sometimes the call gets procrastinated and delayed into a schedule that is only on paper and never gets filled because we refuse to change and grow. Sometimes the person is stubborn and rebellious and only wants her way or no way. The call challenges us to change from a position of prayerlessness to a pattern and habit of prayer.

A call to prayer is, first and foremost, a call to obedience. "Men ought to always pray and not to faint." (Luke 18:1). The call is to born-again believers who have accepted the Lord Jesus Christ into their hearts. They want more than just a causal relationship with our Father. Our spirits are crying for more of God. "As the deer pants after the water brooks, so our soul pants for you, O God." (Psalm 42:6) A call to prayer is the Holy Spirit longing to abide in us in a greater dimension. (John 14:16) God is a Spirit, and I believe He is calling to the spirit within us to come closer, draw nearer, and press for more of His presence in our life.

A call to prayer is a call to a disciplined and committed lifestyle; it is a made-up mind that you are not returning to the way it used to be. A determination and a steadfast spirit that keeps pressing toward the goal. Someone once said, "whatever is gained in prayer must also be maintained in prayer." In other words, prayer doesn't cease!

You know you are hungry for more of God when you hear the clarion call for more. 'In His presence is fullness of joy!" (Psalm 16:11) And you also know that prayer is the avenue by which you can quench that thirst and desire for more.

A call to prayer is to restore the broken fellowship we once experienced with God our Father. It is making that connection that was missing and keeping us in a holding pattern, like an airplane that is made to circle a city repeatedly until it is safe to land. We want to land on our purpose and destiny by heeding the prayer call.

A call to prayer is realizing that it is not the responsibility of a hand full of prayer warriors to lift up your needs and requests to the Lord. It is your responsibility and place to be in a position to stand in the gap on behalf of your family, church, city, and nation. (Luke 10:19) NIV states: "I have given you authority to trample on snakes and scorpions and to overcome all the power of the enemy; nothing will harm you." Hallelujah! We need to just believe the Word of God and act on what He says.

The devil knows when believers come together on one accord to pray, we are a force to be reckoned with. One of the tricks that the devil puts on us is deceiving us into thinking that we don't need to pray. (1 Thessalonians 5:17) Says: "Pray without ceasing." God expects us to be people of prayer.

Prayer is not something that you have an option to decide whether it fits into your schedule. It is supposed to be a daily habit we progressively grow in. That is one of the reasons the devil tries to keep us in darkness concerning prayer. He keeps us busy with the cares of this life, with the deceitfulness of riches. He keeps us busy with offenses and resentment that lingers for months and years.

When we are entertaining and embracing a spirit of fear, we are also in an unripe position of Christianity. Many other demonic spirits keep us in our comfort zones of life and blind us from seeing the accurate picture. 1 John 4:18 states: "There is no fear in love. The one who fears is not made perfect in love." But perfect love drives out fear because fear has to do with punishment. Perfect love cast out the spirit of fear.

If truthful and honest, we should confess that we have not been faithful to the Lord in prayer. If we ask the Lord to forgive us for our prayerlessness and to forgive us for our casual attitude and apathy toward prayer, we must repent. If we ask the Lord to forgive us for our lazy, complacent spirit and ask the Lord to forgive us for making excuses why we can't pray with the saints of God, we must repent.

Acts 3:19 (ASV) states: "Repent ye therefore, and turn again, that your sins may be blotted out, that so there may come seasons of refreshing from the presence of the Lord;" It really is a no-brainer; either our flesh is ruling us, or we are led by the Spirit of God! Revelation 4:16 states, "So then because thou art lukewarm, and neither cold nor hot, I will spue thee out of my mouth." We should really consider this verse as we are repenting. Get beyond the barrier of public sentiments or thoughts people have of you. And grow beyond the blockade of fear that stifles our aspirations.

CHAPTER TWO

ADDRESSING OUR ATTITUDE TOWARD PRAYER

Our approach and attitude to prayer have a lot to do with our demeanor or behavior as we come within range of making up our minds to pray. Our casual, laid-back posture keeps us in an indefinite position of bondage. Some may say that it is the spirit of apathy at play. Others may say it is a spirit of complacency. The traits of that spirit are the absence of passion or emotion or even excitement towards prayer.

Often that spirit of complacency can give you a false sense of security. You are unaware of the danger lurking around the corner, as the devil constantly throws out punches to keep you blinded from his tactics and schemes. Unless you are in a spiritual alert mode, watching and praying, the devil can side-swipe you before you even perceive what is happening. In other words, there must be a desire in the interior section of your heart, a longing, a craving for more of God.

Your desire is what propels you. It's what urges and drives you to seek out this yearning inside of you. You may say to yourself, "Lord, I know there's more! I just want more!" Or you may say like Moses, "Lord, show me Your glory!" God honored that request by hiding Moses in the cleft of the rock, and Moses saw His back parts. (Exodus 33:18-23) This desire forces you to confront this hunger and thirsting of your soul. We must confess that we haven't always been praying as the Word of God commands us. The outcry from our hearts should be, "Lord, give me the right attitude and change the way I think and feel about prayer." Even with the outcry of our hearts, we are praying. "Lord, give me a desire to pray and turn that desire into a passion for praying."

The Word says, unless we come to God in a childlike manner, He won't hear us. Can you imagine coming to God with an arrogant attitude? Suppose we are in positions of power and authority. We must constantly level down or small ourselves up to approach God in prayer. And then level up to get back to our professional positions of power. Our ranting and raving about our needs come nowhere close to bringing God's attention.

Coming to God with a childlike, humble, submissive spirit gets you on a path to approaching Him with the proper mindset.

The spirit and the attitude of the Pharisees still exist in our day. Their arrogant and prideful posture speaks volumes about what they think prayer should be. They believe because they sit in high places, are educated, and make a certain amount of money, they can bypass coming to God in a childlike manner. Everything they do is done for people to see. They love to be greeted with respect. They think that their character and motive for prayer don't matter. When in fact, it makes all the difference in the world.

One of the first things that were said by a Pharisee; "God, I thank you that I'm not like other people, robbers, evildoers, adulterers — or even like this tax collector. I fast twice a week and give a tenth of all I get." (Luke 18:11-12 NIV) This religious man was lacking humility big time! The Pharisee thought he was perfect and didn't need God's help.

One of the primary reasons your prayers don't go any further than the ceiling is because we are arrogant. We think we are more than we are. It's not who we are, it's not what position we hold, it's not how regal we are dressed, and it's not comparing yourself to others that get your prayers heard. But it is a humble, contrite, remorseful, and repentant spirit.

We are proud and possess a spirit of self-importance. We feel as though we are entitled to a particular way of life, a certain lifestyle. This Pharisee first said, "I thank you that I'm not like other people"! What! Can you even imagine someone standing beside you with such a haughty spirit? This man's nerve and audacity to think he is better than everyone else. You almost feel like saying: "Who died and made you king?"

Addressing our personal attitudes in prayer can be quite challenging if we are in positions of authority. I believe that (2 Chronicles 7:14 NIV) gives us a priority or a prerequisite in addressing our approach and demeanor in prayer. "If my people, who are called by my name, will humble themselves and pray and seek my face and turn from their wicked ways, then I will hear from heaven, and I will forgive their sin and will heal their land."

The actual act of becoming a believer is a humbling one. Of which I personally will never forget my own personal experience of salvation. Humility is a character trait, a distinguishing quality that takes a lot of time and effort to develop. It takes some stages of humility to come to God. It's humbling to confess that you believe that there was a man that lived on this earth named Jesus. And that Jesus died and rose from the dead for me. It's humbling to confess all your sins, everything you could think of, that you did wrong. It's humbling to admit your need for Jesus in your life. And then thank Him for accepting you. The first two verbs in that scripture, humble and pray, take time to process and develop as we grow in Christ. It's not just something that just appears on the scene. Then "boom," we have it. It takes humility to admit that you have been operating in pride. It takes humility to develop character.

Many people quote 2 Chronicles 7:14 without really thinking about their own lack of humility, that hinders their prayers. If we are believers, born-again, (Christians), or kingdom citizens, then prayer should not be foreign to us. Prayer is a part of who we are! Prayer is like the air we breathe. Prayer is our interaction with God. Prayer is simply talking with God and God talking to you. It's a real relationship with our Father.

Moses was more humble than anyone else on the face of the earth. (Numbers 12:3 NIV) Another version says: (AMP) Moses was very meek, gentle, kind, and humble. The word 'meek' is described in the dictionary as 'overly submissive! Many will respond, "Well, we can pack our bags and go home now. Because I'm not going to be overly submissive to anyone." Why am I mentioning Moses, you may ask? Moses was also known as an intercessor. He prayed a lot and interceded. He stood in the gap on behalf of others. Just look at the numerous times he went back and forth to God on behave of the Israelites. The times he cried out to God for understanding and clarity.

We, believers, must stop drawing a line in the sand. And declaring we will never reach higher levels because of our lack of growth or refusal to grow and mature.

When we think about changing and addressing our attitude toward prayer, one of the significant players of resistance is pride! Pride will keep you locked up in a maximum prison, only to give you one hour a day of fresh air. Pride keeps you wrapped in yourself; you don't realize that other people are in the room. Pride will keep invisible blinders over your eyes so that everyone can see you but you. Pride can keep you in bondage for years until you hear and accept the truth about yourself. And even then, it has to fight to get an acknowledgment that you don't know everything.

In examining our attitude towards prayer, I believe that the spirit of humility comes knocking at our door every so often to get us to think about someone else and their concerns. Humility takes time to develop in a believer's life and a conscious commitment or awareness of the season of Christian growth God has us in.

What made Moses the humblest man on earth and overly submissive to God's process? Was it because he was raised as a prince in Egypt for 40 years? Was it because he was a shepherd in Midian for 40 years? Or was it being the Leader, Lawgiver, and Intercessor of the Israelites? I believe that through all the assignments God gave Moses, He saw his heart and obedience to simply do what God told him to do.

Getting past the hindrance of Moses not believing that he was able to be used to speak to the Israelites was a major weakness or disability that prevented Moses from operating to his full ability, to just believing God. When we look at our own skills, we are convinced that it can't be done. Only when we stop looking at what we can accomplish, in our strength, and look to God will the impossible become possible!

I absolutely love the attitude of Moses when he said, "If your Presence doesn't go with us, don't send us from this place." (Exodus 33:15) Wow! Look at the progression of Moses' demeanor. Lord, if You, Your presence, doesn't go with me, don't let me budge from this place. How often have we challenged our positions to move because of our flesh? Our flesh was speaking louder than our spirit.

How many times has God said to us, "be still and let Me give the signal to move." How often have we moved ahead of God, only to find disaster in our circumstances at the end of the day. Our attitude, willingness, and surrendering to God's process to follow Christ hinges on our ability to follow instructions.

When addressing our attitude towards prayer, the finger of blaming others for our incompetence should be pointed at ourselves. Remember, Jesus, said, "some thirty, some sixty, and some a hundred." God doesn't make you live on a higher level; He gives us a choice.

What do we do with the Word that comes forth concerning prayer? Do we ignore or apply the Word to ourselves? That decision is totally left up to you. It's growth when you begin to examine yourself as to why you're not maturing in prayer. And it is growth when you start to take steps in humbling yourself before God.

Our behavior can be a barrier as we challenge ourselves to confront our mindsets toward prayer. Our sincere prayer should be, "Lord help me not to turn a deaf ear to your clarion call to pray. Give me ears to hear what the Spirit of the Lord is saying, and apply myself to your Word, In Jesus Name."

CHAPTER THREE

THE PRINCIPLES OF PRAYER

As you pursue your desire for more intimacy with our Father through prayer, important principles will guide you into a more prosperous and influential prayer life. Principles are guidelines or rules that help keep you productive and progressive in prayer. Guidelines keep you from veering off into the left field. Sometimes we hear other believers praying, and we may say to ourselves, "wow, they can really pray." And we may pick up some of the exact verbiages because it sounded good and got audible results. That thought can get you into a lot of trouble and wasted time. I have found that keeping within the rails of the principles of prayer is where I see most of my results in prayer. Picking up a sequence of words to sound like we have it together is risky and immature. When you have an authentic experience with the Lord, you don't want a fake display of His presence in your life. I want to be that vessel the Holy Spirit can use to accomplish His plans and visions. And that can't be effectively done if I'm still playing games or even not ready to be used by God.

God is looking for available arteries through which His Word can flow unhindered. If you are still at the stage where it doesn't matter whether we pray, this book is probably not for you.

Principles That Work

1. **Make up your mind that you will be faithful to Him no matter what.** (Psalm 101:6) Mine eyes shall be upon the faithful of the land, that they may dwell with me: he that walketh in a perfect way, he shall serve me. Let God see your hunger and thirst for more of Him in your life. Let the record show your faithfulness to Him. This decision does not come lightly. When you say yes to God, it will seem like all hell is breaking loose.

If you are straddling the fence, which means, you are partly in the church and partly in the world, then your mind is not made up. The devil will make up an excuse for you that you're not ready. The devil hates a person that possesses a steadfast spirit toward God. But guess what, the opposite of committing is being in a state of complacency. You're unaware of the devil's traps he is setting up for your downfall. You may even feel satisfied everything in your life is going well.

2. **Be determined to seek His Face only.** Hunger and long for more of Him. (1 Chronicles 16:11) Seek

the Lord and his strength. Seek his face continually. Don't let people get you off from seeking God's face. When you are determined, nothing will be able to sway you in one direction or another. Being relentless means, you have a conviction in your inner man and are dedicated to seeking Him.

No matter what is going on in your life, you make a beeline back to seeking His face. (Matt. 5:6) Blessed are they which do hunger and thirst after righteousness for they shall be filled. It's a constant resolute stirring on the inside of you. You must have more of Him. In His presence is fullness of joy. The Holy Spirit's presence fills you with so much reassurance and blessings you feel like just remaining there to soak in more of His presence. And then you are grateful for His affirmation in your life.

3. **Appreciate Him for what He is doing in your life.** (Psalm 118:6) The Lord is on my side; I will not fear: what can man do unto me? Realize that God is blessing you right now. Where would I be if it had not been for the Lord on my side? Appreciating our Father is the attitude we should possess and making it a habit of being grateful for all the things He has done in our lives. Enjoying God should dominate our lifestyle.

When the reality of life provokes you, and you realize it's God keeping you alive, your gratitude and thankfulness go to another level. (Psalm 34:1) I will bless the Lord at all times: his praise shall continually be in my mouth. Sometimes we take the small things for granted. It's not until the small things are not functioning that we appreciate them.

4. **Worship Him for who He is.** (John 4:23-24) But the hour cometh, and now is, when the true worshippers shall worship the Father in Spirit and in truth: for the Father seeketh such to worship him. God is a Spirit: and they that worship him must worship him in spirit and in truth. When we worship Him, our eyes are off ourselves and upon Him. Think about who He is and what He's done for you. Bow down and worship Him. True worship comes from the heart. Why do you think David cried out to God and said, "Create in me a clean heart, O God; and renew a right spirit within me." (Ps. 51:10)

We can't give ourselves a new heart. Only God can do that. Worry and worship can't function at the same time. We must be worshippers. If we want to see more of our prayers answered, live a life of worship to Him. (Psalm 29:2) Give unto the Lord the glory due unto his name; worship the Lord in the beauty of holiness. Even when you don't feel like it, worship Him. Speak to your flesh and declare that you will worship Him with every breath He gives you.

5. **Be specific in your prayer request.** And don't complain about His timing. (Rom. 8:28) And we know that all things work together for good to them who

are called according to his purpose. When you are specific, you are clarifying your request. It's not just a vague "Lord, touch, Lord, bless, Lord, walk by." When we pray specifically, it increases our faith. When we really get a revelation of who God is and how much He loves us, we then understand that He does all things well.

All things mean all things. Everything that appears upon your front door; God has allowed. God looks at the complete picture of our lives, then permits or blocks. He doesn't need our help, and He doesn't need our permission. When we complain about our circumstances, it only means that we haven't learned our lesson yet. And we probably need to take the test over again.

6. **Live a life of holiness, righteousness, and integrity.** (1 Peter 1:15-16) But as he which hath called you is holy, so be ye holy in all manner of conversation; because it is written, Be ye holy; for I am holy. We are called to live a holy life. He called us with a holy calling. Living holy means, we live a life set apart, reserved to glorify God.

It is a life of discipline. (Ephesians 6:14) Stand therefore, having your loins girt about with truth, and having on the breastplate of righteousness. Righteousness is being in right standing with God. Jesus as the Son of God is God's gift to us when we believe. And integrity is living in truth. Your Word is your bond. Being a man/woman of holiness is a spiritual peculiarity that distinguishes you from others. Your character speaks volumes before you even say a word. Walking in integrity boost your prayers.

7. **Don't do all the talking; be still and listen.** (Psalm 46:10) Be still and know that I am God: I will be exalted among the heathen, I will be exalted in the earth. God is not interested in much talking. He is interested in us listening and obeying Him. God often wants us just to be still; because He has us. Be confident that He who began a good work in you will carry it on to completion until the day of Christ Jesus. (Philippians 1:6) I believe that God is always talking and revealing things to us all the time. But we aren't in tune with what He is saying because we are too busy.

8. **Believe in God's Word.** (Mark 9:23) Jesus said unto him, "If thou canst believe, all things are possible to him that believeth." God just simply asks us to believe His Word. Don't try to reason it out and explain it, just believe. Many times, we try to put reasoning into why God does what He does.

God is sovereign. End of the story. One man cried out, "Lord help my unbelief." All things are possible according to God's will. His will and purpose for your life play a significant part.

9. **Operate in faith.** (Hebrews 11:6) But without faith it is impossible to please him: for he that cometh to God must believe that he is and that he is a rewarder of them that diligently seek him. Faith hopes for what it can't see. Faith opens the door of belief and encourages it to move. One of the areas that Jesus fussed at the disciples after He rose from the dead was their unbelief and their hardness of heart. Our position is to take the first step of faith. Don't be afraid to do what seems like the impossible. (Matthew 19:26) But Jesus beheld them and said unto them, "With men this is impossible, but with God all things are possible." God asks us to do what seems, in our eyes, impossible. He just wants someone to use, to do the impossible. So that He gets the glory.

10. **Commit and consecrate your life to Him.** (John 17:19 AMP) And so for their sake and on their behalf, I sanctify, dedicate, consecrate Myself, that they also may be sanctified, dedicated, consecrated, made holy in the Truth. Our lifestyle can't be in and out of the world when we try to get closer to Him. Our lives can't be faltering.

When you consecrate yourself, you are strengthening your position for God to answer your prayers. As you grow in Christ, you get tired of all the foolishness and the games people play. God doesn't work on our time schedule. We are called to be available to His time schedule.

11. **Be persistent and persevere in the spirit.** Being persistent means; you are not playing and are serious about the situation. Don't get tired, don't give up, and don't give in. Persevere, and maintain. Be steadfast, unmovable, always abounding in the work of the Lord, for as much as you know your labor is not in vain. (1 Corinthians 15:58)

The spirit of perseverance and determination will win every time, according to God's will. Luke 11:1-8 testifies of a shameless, persistent, and insistence person that has made up in their mind to keep on asking until they see results. We give up too quickly.

12. **Don't be moved by what you see with your physical eyes.** The devil will put things or thoughts in your mind to get you to give up or throw in the white towel of surrender. Keep your eyes on Jesus. About midnight, Paul and Silas were praying and singing hymns to God, and the other prisoners were listening to them. (Acts 16:25)

The circumstances surrounding Paul and Silas were devastating; there was no way they were getting out of their predicament. They didn't look at their physical condition. They were severely beaten, put in the inner cell, and their feet were in chains. But, Hallelujah, they began giving praise to God. And God worked a miracle.

13. **In everything, give thanks.** (1 Thessalonians 5:18 NIV) Give thanks in all circumstances, for this is God's will for you in Christ Jesus. Be thankful and grateful for what and how God is orchestrating and composing your life. Give thanks in every situation.

When you are giving thanks to God, you say, Lord, I trust you! It's God's will to give thanks in every condition. His love for us is so great that He won't allow anything in our life that will harm us.

14. **Confess your consistent need for Him.** But seek first his kingdom and his righteousness, and all these things will also be given to you. (Matt. 6:33) We can't live, breathe, or move without Him in our life. Realize your constant need for our Father in your life. We need His guidance throughout our daily lives.

He is the one that gently warns us about the storms that are swirling ahead. He is the one that cautions us to pump the breaks in certain situations.

15. **Repent and turn; repent and turn; repent and turn.** (Acts 3:19 NIV) Repent, then, and turn to God, so that your sins may be wiped out, that times of refreshing may come from the Lord. We never get to where we've "arrived" in our journey of this Christian life. Our life must be a life of repenting and turning, morphing into His image.

Sometimes believers get to the point that they think they don't have to repent, because of their longevity in the Lord. In fact, the definition of repent is, feeling sorry or ashamed for your conduct. Which of us is in a place we do not have to apologize for something we did?

16. **Ask Him for a spirit of humility.** (1 Peter 5:6) Humble yourselves therefore under the mighty hand of God, that he may exalt you in due time. We will not hear some messages unless we possess a humble spirit. Our ears become dull of hearing.

Naaman was a commander in the Syrian army who almost messed up his miracle of being healed from leprosy because of his lack of humility. (2 Kings 5) Appreciate His grace and mercy in your life. (Hebrews 4:16 NIV) Let us then approach God's throne of grace with confidence so that we may receive mercy and find grace to help us in our time of need. Be thankful for His undeserved grace and mercy in your life. Be conscious of His goodness in your life. You don't always have to be the one getting the credit for accomplishments.

17. **Ask the Lord to teach you how to pray.** (Luke 11:1) And it came to pass that as he was praying in a certain place, when he ceased, one of his disciples said unto him, Lord, teach us to pray, as John also taught his disciples. Having a relationship with the Holy Spirit is so valuable. The Holy Spirit is so gentle and sweet. He meets us on our level.

If you let Him, He will strategically lead you to the scriptures you need to guide you along the way. And He (the Holy Ghost) (John 14:26) will teach you.

18. **Keep an alert posture and pray in the spirit.** (Ephesians 6:18 NIV) And pray in the Spirit on all occasions with all kinds of prayers and requests. Be alert and always keep on praying for all the Lord's people. We are called to watch as well as pray. Stay sensitive to what's going on around you. Stay alert to how the devil is trying to get you off point. Stay alert to his demonic traps. Stay alert to his subtle suggestions. Stay alert to last-minute attacks.

An attack that you didn't see coming. The devil loves surprises. And before you know it, you are cursing someone out. He has increased your blood pressure, all because you let your guards down.

19. **Guard the gates of your spirit, your eyes, and you're hearing.** (Proverbs 4:20-23 NIV) My son, pay attention to what I say; turn your ear to my words. Do not let them out of your sight, keep them within your heart; for they are life to those who find them and health to one's whole body. Above all else, guard your heart, for everything you do flows from it. Your spirit is so sensitive; you must protect the things the devil tries to slip in unnoticed.

Your testimony has been affected. If you have female and male friends sleeping together without being married, and you haven't told them what the word says about shacking up. Guard what you allow to come before your eyes. The devil will play that R-rated scene in your spirit when you think you've moved to another level. He'll say, "Hey, remember this?" Guard your ears in what you listen to. Guard your eyes on what you let pass in front of them. And guard your heart because out of the abundance of the heart, the mouth speaks. (Matt. 12:34)

20. **Pray in Jesus's Name.** (John 14:13-14 NIV) And I will do whatever you ask in my name, so that the Father may be glorified in the Son. You may ask me for anything in my name, and I will do it. One of the keys to getting your prayers answered is praying in Jesus's name. We have his authorized permission to use his name according to his will. He wants us to ask in his name that our joy might be full.

Adopting the principles of prayer can usher us to maturity and break the roadblocks of inconsistency.

CHAPTER FOUR

THE WORK OF THE HOLY SPIRIT

While traveling on one of our arduous and challenging journeys to Onitsha, Nigeria, I was grateful and appreciative to our Father that I was filled with the Holy Ghost. The thought of taking our world missions team to Nigeria meant preparing myself mentally and spiritually to be presented with difficulties. We flew into Lagos, Nigeria approximately 1:00pm in the afternoon, with arrangements to fly out of Lagos to Enugu. Soon after we landed and got to our departure gate, an announcement came over the intercom, "the airlines are now on strike." The team members looked at each other in disbelief. Of course, I'm not saying a word because I don't want to alarm them. I am telling myself, "You got to be kidding me." Okay, so now this is serious! We begin to see airline attendants leaving their posts of duty.

As I am regrouping myself, the team leader (my husband) is aggressively conversing with the host about our options. Understand that it is a well-documented fact not to drive in Nigeria after dark. So, we were faced with a dilemma. Either continue to hope and pray that the airlines would come to their senses or consider spending the night in Lagos at the airport.

After waiting two and a half hours at our departure gate, they allowed us to board the plane and fly to Enugu. We are now three hours behind schedule. Our itinerary was planned several months ahead of our trip to arrive in Enugu at three o'clock in the afternoon so we could drive to Onitsha before dark.

Our plane arrived in Enugu, and by this time, we could see diminishing rays of light from the sun setting in the west. One part of me is happy that we could land in Enugu, and the other part is alarmed because it's dark outside. There is another intensive, aggressive meeting between our team leader and the host.

Our host decided to take two cars and drive to Onitsha, about 40 minutes away. Waiting on the vehicles to arrive took us to the edge of darkness. It was pitch black! The reality of that moment slapped me in the face and said: "Girl, you better start praying!" I began praying in the Spirit. As we were getting our luggage situated, my posture was focused. It wasn't the type of prayer that you start off praying; "Now Father, You know our situation, and You know we are here in Enugu." No! In a whisper, I began Praising and Worshipping our Father. I began thanking Him for how He brought us safely to the nation of Nigeria. I started praising Him that nothing was too hard for Him!

Then I stepped over into my prayer language! Hallelujah, thank you, Lord, for my prayer language! My prayer language is praying in the Spirit, praying in other tongues. We were now situated in two cars. I stayed in that prayer position until I noticed a very contentious conversation between our host and driver. They were speaking in their Nigerian dialect, so we couldn't understand a word they were saying. I looked on the road and could see flickering lights on the highway.

As we advanced closer to the flickering lights, we saw firepots on either end of a giant log in the middle of the road. The only way to get out of that entrapment was to not stop. So, we had to drive at a fast speed, partly on the highway and partly on the dirt road, to get past these bandits. Our host encouraged the driver to press his foot flat on the gas pedal. Being from Nigeria he knew it was bandits, but he didn't alert us until the Lord performed a miracle right before our eyes. As we curved from the highway to the dirt swerving back on the highway, we could see the bandits coming out from the thick darkness of the trees, yelling and throwing rocks and sticks at us to get us to stop the car. What a mighty God we serve! He delivered us from the hands of the bandits!

I believe that as I was praying in the Holy Ghost (in the Spirit), the Lord was using me to pray His perfect will for that situation. I didn't know what danger was up ahead, but He did. And that's the beauty of praying in the Spirit.

A handful of unforgettable, significant occasions marked a change in my life. The first was accepting and giving my life to Jesus. The second was getting married seven months after going on a blind date to the love of my life. The third, one of the most memorable landmark events in my life, is the moment the Lord baptized and filled me with the Holy Ghost.

It was a life-changing, exhilarating, and eye-opening experience that transformed and adjusted my whole perspective of my Christian consciousness. Physically, I wanted to do cartwheels across the Saint Augustine grass in my front yard. Yes, well, you know that wasn't going to happen. But spiritually, my spirit was leaping for joy. The work of the Holy Spirit operating in a believer's life can be one of the most rewarding experiences in their life.

When I think about the precious Holy Spirit in my life, my question is: "How did I maintain without it?" And on the other hand, there are many challenges of being filled with the Holy Spirit. But we will talk about that later.

We know that the Holy Spirit is part of the Godhead, the trinity, Father, Son, & Holy Spirit. We pray to our Father in the Name of Jesus. The Holy Spirit is so gentle and kind. As you read this next section of this book, I pray you to keep an open heart as I share my personal experience with the Holy Spirit. We know that the Holy Spirit won't force himself upon you.

The desire and longing I had in my spirit was a pursuit for more of God in my life. I was born again at the age of 22. And even in that experience, it took a week of me seeking God day and night until I felt a physical and spiritual change at the end of the seven days. It was a marked change. It was an awareness of my body being brand new! I remember calling my Father, saying, "Daddy, I'm really born again!" I was so excited about my transformation that I wanted to tell everyone I encountered that I was born again. And I felt the Spirit of God in my life.

Many years later, God began to draw my attention to prayer. I didn't know much about the subject of prayer, only that I knew God was calling me to learn more about intimacy with Him. My quest for more of Him grew into a hunger and a thirst. And within my spirit, I could feel that there was more. I was born again, yes! I was in the church, yes! My life was changed, yes! But there was more. I began searching the scriptures. I got hung up on the scripture that said, "And these signs shall follow them that believe; In my Name shall they cast out devils; they shall speak with new tongues; They shall take up serpents; and if they drink any deadly thing, it shall not hurt them; they shall lay hands on the sick, and they shall recover." (Mark 16:17-18) This scripture right here messed me up real good! The 18th verse started with these words; "And these signs shall follow them that believe;" I said, "Well I believe, and I don't cast out devils, and I don't speak in tongues!" Can you imagine my mindset and my inner struggle in a Baptist church? The odds are stacked against me. But God kept calling me to go with Him deeper.

The following scriptures that gave me pause were (Acts 2:3-4) And there appeared unto them cloven tongues like as of fire, and it sat upon each of them. And they were all filled with the Holy Ghost, and began to speak with tongues, as the Spirit gave them utterance. These were 120 believers in one place, in an upper room, on the day of Pentecost, and they were all filled with the Holy Ghost. Wow! I couldn't possibly stop my search of the scriptures now. Too many things were happening.

This scripture didn't say a select few received the Holy Ghost; it said, "they were all filled." They were there because Jesus told them to wait for the promise of the Father. ... "but ye shall be baptized with the Holy Ghost not many days hence." (Acts 1:4-5) Some scholars believe it was 10 days before that promise was fulfilled. Can you even envision the thoughts going on in their heads? After day six, seven, or eight, can you see them asking, "how long we got to be in this upper room?' They may have even asked, "We believe that Jesus is the Son of God; what more do we need?" And I believe Peter may have tried to talk a few of them into going fishing! (Acts 1:8 NIV) "But you will receive power when the Holy Spirit comes on you, and you will be my witnesses in Jerusalem, and in all Judea and Samaria, and to the ends of the earth." If you doubt it ended there, it didn't stop there.

The Apostles were in Jerusalem and heard that Samaria had received the Word of God. Philip was proclaiming the gospel of the kingdom of God and the name of Jesus. They believed and were baptized, both men and women. They sent Peter and John to Samaria.

When they arrived, they prayed for the new believers that they might receive the Holy Spirit.

Now get this part; just hearing the gospel preached, believing that Jesus is your Lord and Savior, and even getting baptized was not enough. The Apostles wanted them to have the whole experience. Many of us in our personal journey of accepting Christ stop right there. I know because I was one of them. And I could feel the sweet Holy Spirit moving in my life. From time to time, the Lord would put clapping in my hands, or I would just weep before the Lord when His presence would come on me.

I find it amazing that in Acts 8:16, that verse says, "because the Holy Spirit had not yet come on any of them; they had simply been baptized in the name of the Lord Jesus." Do you mean to tell me that just accepting Jesus and getting baptized wasn't all of it?

Now, in my eyes, that was a problem. I felt like saying, "You mean to tell me all this time I've been a Christian, and nobody told me about being filled with the Holy Ghost"! You might even say; I wasn't ready for the Holy Ghost. The sole purpose of Peter and John was to pray for them that they would receive the Holy Ghost. So, they prayed, laid their hands on them, and they received the Holy Ghost.

After all those years of being saved, the Word of God really didn't explode inside of me until I began to hunger and thirst and search for more of God's presence.

To further my excitement and study about the Holy Spirit, in (Acts 10:44-47), God is dealing with Peter about the Jewish law. Peter is preaching and proclaims that he now knows that God does not show favoritism. Still, every person who fears him and does righteousness is acceptable. He goes on to testify of the ministry of Jesus and how they crucified him and how He rose from the dead. Now just think about this subsequent circumstance of events. Let it marinate in your spirit.

While Peter was still speaking, the Holy Spirit came down on all those who heard the message. The men who accompanied Peter were astonished that the Holy Spirit had been poured out on the Gentiles. They heard them speaking in other tongues and declaring the greatness of God. Why was this so astonishing to them? Because they thought that the Holy Spirit was only for the Jews.

The final nail in the coffin, so to speak for me, was found in (Acts 19:1-6). Paul travels to Ephesus and finds some disciples. The first question he asks them is, "Did you receive the Holy Spirit when you believed?" Their answer may surprise you. They said, "We haven't even heard that there is a Holy Spirit!" Paul was amazed by their response and asked, "Then what baptism were you baptized?" They said, "With John's baptism." Paul responded, "John's baptized with a baptism of repentance. "In short, after their conversation, they were baptized in the Name of the Lord Jesus, and Paul laid hands on them. They began to speak in other languages and prophesy.

Some groups tell you that you must speak in tongues before you can even be considered as being born again. I know that is not true because I was born again for years before I was filled or baptized with the

Holy Ghost. In my experience, I was longing for more of God's presence in my life. Please understand me, the Word of God says in (Romans 10:9-10 CSV), "If you confess with your mouth, Jesus is Lord, and believe in your heart that God raised Him from the dead, You Will Be Saved. With the heart, one believes, resulting in righteousness, and with the mouth, one confesses, resulting in salvation."

In my quest for more of God, it wasn't just a casual inquiry. It wasn't just an "in the moment" idea; this was a reoccurring episode awakening my spirit of seeking His face.

Your hunger and your passion for the things of God dictate the outcome. If you have a feeble and weak petition, asking God for more, then I'm afraid that will be what you receive.

God wants to see if you are serious about your desire and appeal. The Word says: "Ask and it will be given you; seek, and you will find; knock, and the door will be opened to you: For everyone who asks receives; the one who seeks finds; and to the one who knocks, the door will be opened. Which of you, if your son asks for bread, will give him a stone? Or if he asks for a fish, will give him a snake? If you, then, though you are evil, know how to give good gifts to your children, how much more will your Father in heaven give good gifts to those who ask him." (Matthew 7:7-11 NIV) Our faith is essential to getting our prayers answered, which we will discuss later. Changing my perspective, my viewpoint of the Holy Spirit operating in a greater dimension broke barriers in my life.

CHAPTER FIVE

THE WORK OF THE HOLY SPIRIT PART TWO

The work of the Holy Spirit in my life became very crucial. I began to see myself growing in self-confidence and courage towards prayer. I was building myself up in the Holy Ghost. (Jude 1:20 NIV) But you, dear friends, by building yourselves up in your most holy faith and praying in the Holy Spirit. I began to look forward to my times of prayer with my Father.

As I committed to prayer times, the Lord began to reveal things to me, and He began to speak to me more. How sweet and precious was my time in the presence of the Lord. Then I began to see how demonic forces were doing everything in their power, to keep me from praying and spending time in the word. A television program, a phone call, a shopping trip, a word puzzle, anything would come up to derail my commitment to pray.

The devil would convince me that I was too tired or sleepy to pray. He would try to take me into custody and shackle my mind with deceptions and lies. The devil tried to restrain me with hurts and past wounds. He tried to capture the gates of my eyes by showing elicit R-rated scenes on tv. The devil will try, by any means necessary, to get me to back off my prayer life.

One of my concerns about prayer before being filled with the Holy Spirit was being able to pray longer than ten or fifteen minutes in one setting. You know how those prayers go; "Lord bless my husband, bless my children, bless my siblings, bless my mama and my daddy, bless my church, bless the Pastor, bless my friends, and Lord bless me, Amen." "Oh, and Lord bless the Mayor, bless the Governor, and bless the President of these United States of America." That prayer took five minutes to pray.

When you are filled with the Spirit, you take a prayer request to God and pray in your native tongue as much as you know about the concern, and then you go into your prayer language. Praying in the Spirit doesn't always mean that you pray in tongues. Praying in the Spirit also means that you are praying the heart of God, and you are led by the Spirit of God. You don't have to be filled with the Spirit to pray the heart of God. But it sure helps.

Not long after, I was filled with the Spirit, speaking in other tongues; I transitioned into singing in the Spirit. Singing in the Spirit helped me when I was in difficult situations where I could not just get on my face before the Lord and cry out. In a low alto voice, I would just begin to sing to Him in the Spirit.

Many years ago, on one of our World Missions trips, before the airlines started having direct flights into certain nations, we flew from Los Angeles to London and to Cote d'Ivoire, the (Ivory Coast) Abidjan.

When we arrived in the morning at about 11:00am, the announcement was made that the flight at 3:00pm we were booked on to fly into Mozambique was packed, and we would have to wait until the next day to fly out. We were tired, and we didn't get all our sleep on the plane, and now in this foreign country, everybody is speaking French, it's sweltering, and every person is clamoring in this small space at the front desk to get out! Lord have mercy!

My husband looks at me and says, "Doll pray, there's no way we're going to get on this next plane." At that moment, I was so grateful to have my prayer language. The level of aggressiveness and hostile attitudes hovering around that small space was almost unbearable. Not to mention the closeness of our bodies pressing against each other, trying to maneuver our way out. Yelling, shouting, and pushing to get to the front of the line was a zealous thought. We clutched our bags to ensure we weren't being picked-pocketed by the onslaught of French-speaking people.

Again, my husband looks at me and says: "Pray, Doll!" Even though it was a French-speaking nation, I felt good about praying in the Spirit because I knew I could see us getting on that airplane. Even though everything around us said, we were stuck like Chuck.

We got on the airplane. We were the last two names called. They were middle seats, but we got out! And it looked impossible, but God! My prayer position was not a loud, boisterous and intense standing but a strong and determined resolute that God would come through on the request. I was praying softly and just under my breath. On the outside, you could see my lips moving, but not able to understand what was being said; that was for the Father. And on the inside, warring in the spirit.

Prayer and the word of God go hand in hand. In some instances, I would remind the Lord of what He said in His Word. I would say, "Lord, You said that You would supply all my needs according to Your riches in glory: and I'm standing on that promise. Lord, You said that Faith comes by hearing and hearing by the Word of God. Lord help me to read and meditate on Your Word." Being filled with the Holy Spirit means we must keep God's Word in our hearts.

Praying in the Holy Spirit helps you pray more effectively on behalf of others. There are times when I am praying in the Spirit, and the Lord reveals to me the demonic spirits that need to be bound. Or He may reveal the truth of a particular situation.

I can't tell you the numerous times the Holy Spirit has come to my rescue that encouraged my spirit. The gift of the Holy Spirit is connected with prayer. When Jesus started His ministry, he was praying, and the Holy Spirit descended on Him. (Luke 3:21-22 NIV) "When all the people were being baptized, Jesus was baptized too. And as he was praying, heaven was opened, and the Holy Spirit descended on him in bodily form like a dove. And a voice came from heaven: "You are my Son, whom I love; with you, I am well pleased." The word of God says: that Jesus was full of the Holy Spirit before He went on His 40 days fast.

To me, it's fascinating to know that there are some believers that are so full of pride and arrogancy to think they have enough common sense to accomplish specific tasks without consulting God first. It is not our strategic planning that boosts us into positions, but it is our availability and humility to God's timing so that He gets the glory.

When we say we want to be like Jesus, it is more than just a notion. Let's begin by starting our ministries with prayer. Let's kick off our ministries by perfecting the area of holiness in our lives. Let's start by getting instructions from our Heavenly Father. Let's practice being humble and submissive to leadership. Let's operate in a spirit of love and compassion. Trying to do it on our own will cause you to run into a brick wall every time.

Before Jesus made significant decisions, He would spend His nights in prayer. It also intrigued me that Jesus' disciples asked him how to pray. Out of all the things that Jesus was doing, the one thing they inquired about was praying. They didn't ask Jesus to teach them how to multiply the loaves of bread and fish. They didn't ask Jesus how to open blind eyes. They didn't ask Jesus how to raise the dead! They asked Jesus how to pray! It was evident that prayer played a major role in Jesus' life.

I believe it is of utmost importance that we are presented with the full picture of what gifts concerning prayer are given to us as believers. I grew up in a Baptist church, but I didn't give my life to Christ until I was 22 years old.

My mother played the organ every Sunday for the choir. My Father was the head of the Deacon Board for years. We were practically in Church almost every day of the week, with different meetings. My siblings always told me that when you grow up, you're going to be a Holiness Believer, a Church of God in Christ Saint. They said that because I loved going to Church so much.

All those years in the Church, I went through the religious motions, but I did not accept Jesus into my heart. I loved the Sunday school, I loved the youth department, I loved the usher's board, and I loved church fellowships.

I shared all my experiences with you because I believe many of us are just going through religious movements. Sometimes we get stuck in one place because we really don't want to be bothered. We are happy where we are, going to heaven, and that's enough.

I couldn't let go of certain scriptures. In Mark 1:8, it says: John the Baptist is talking; "I indeed have baptized you with water: but he shall baptize you with the Holy Ghost." The water part I understood, but the baptize you with the Holy Ghost; that's where I began searching the scriptures. I realized that there is a difference between the gift of tongues and the gift of the Holy Spirit.

I shied away from tongues because people always said, "you have to have an interpreter if you speak out loud in tongues." During my search on tongues, I discovered that there is a difference. My main interest was in my personal prayer time. It wasn't my goal to try and impress someone with my prayer language. Paul said, "I thank God, I speak with tongues more than all of you. But in the Church, I would rather speak five intelligible words to instruct others than ten thousand words in a tongue! (1 Corinthians 14:18-19. NIV) I'm also reminded of the word that says, "If I speak in the tongues of men or of angels, but do not have love, I am only a resounding gong or a clanging cymbal." (1 Cor. 13:1 NIV) I can't get so carried away in praying in tongues that I don't operate in the Spirit of love. My personal prescription that involved a regular communion with the Holy Spirit broke boundaries and shifted my spiritual growth to another level.

CHAPTER SIX

YOUR JOURNEY OF PRAYER

Beginning your journey of prayer can be refreshing as well as exhilarating. There must be a determination, a dogmatic spirit that refuses to give up on the inside of your spirit, that craves and hungers for more of God's presence in your life more than anything. There must be a longing, a passion for having that intimate relationship where you feel and know without a doubt that He is with you.

It is a keen sense of awareness in your spirit that out of all the issues that confront you in this life; you know in your spirit; that this is not it. Your connection to the Spirit of God addresses the questions within your spirit. It's not just going through the motions of what you've learned over the years about using your religious language when it is appropriate. "Hallelujah, Thank You Jesus; God is good, all the time, and all the time; God is good, and I'm blessed and highly favored." All the while you're hurting on the inside. Can you really say: "I'm too blessed to be stressed," without going throughout the rest of the day complaining about your situation? No! Please don't misunderstand me; we get so used to our religious language that it no longer has an impact on the hearers.

"Lord, I'm not moving from my position until I confidently and assuredly hear from You," which is easier said than done. In this season of prayer and submission that God is calling you to, your journey must be determined, strong and aggressive to arrest and take captive the attitude of seeing results and spiritual growth within yourself. You must be persistent and firm to confess: "God it's all about You and where You want to take me." Your journey in prayer must take precedence, and it must take priority above everything else. It must be the engine that drives my actions. In other words, God is First and foremost. He is not an afterthought, He is First! God is not to be put at the end of the day when I'm tired and worn out. He desires and deserves more from us than that. Don't give Him the leftovers, when you're ready to retire.

When you begin to engage yourself and devote and adjust your spirit accordingly, putting Him first becomes second nature. I can't imagine being so caught up in life that I ignore the one that is responsible for my very existence. Lord, forgive us for being so self-centered and narrow-minded. We breathe, live, and survive solely because God is Good! Not because we have been so good, but God is good to the just and the unjust alike. (Matthew 5:45)

My first response to the Lord before I even get out of bed, when I open my eyes in the morning, is, "Good

Morning My Father, Good Morning Lord, Jesus, Good Morning Holy Spirit. Thank You, Lord, for another day."

Our pattern for prayer is the Lord's Prayer found in Matthew 6:9-13. The subject of prayer in this chapter starts with verse five, and Jesus admonishes us on what not to do when we are praying. "Don't stand in the churches and street corners to be seen by others when you pray. Don't multiply words, repeating the same ones over and over again. But this is what you are to do; go into your room, close the door, and pray to your Father, who is unseen. Then your Father, who sees what is done in secret, will reward you."

Our pattern for prayer, our guidance, our direction, or you might say, our outline for prayer, is found in Matthew 6 & Luke 11. It's called the Lord's Prayer.

STEP ONE: <u>One of the first things that you need to know in prayer is that you address Our Father in Jesus' Name.</u> We acknowledge our Father. (John 16:23-24) "In that day you will no longer ask me anything. Very truly I tell you, my Father will give you whatever you ask in my name. Until now you have not asked for anything in my name. Ask and you will receive, and your joy will be complete." The letters are in red, so that tells me Jesus is speaking. He is telling them to pray in His Name.

When we learn how to pray, we address Our Father in Jesus' Name. We are acknowledging Our Father. Whatever you feel the most comfortable with when you approach the throne, you address our Father in Jesus' name. For example, Dear Heavenly Father; Precious Father; Father God; Father; Oh Lord God Our

Father; Eternal God Our Father; Abba Father; Father we stretch our hands to you; Gracious God Our Father; Almighty God Our Father; Sovereign Lord, and King.

When we acknowledge Our Father, we are addressing Him. We must give our first attention to Our Father. He is our Loving, Heavenly Father. Our Father is in heaven, and He hears us when we pray. It is inappropriate and not fitting just casually to come to Our Father without first addressing Our Father. When we first address our Father, we pray according to God's word.

Coming before our Father without first acknowledging him would be like your child coming to you to ask for something. As a parent, you couldn't imagine one of your children coming up to you and immediately start asking you for money or the car, or your cell phone, or tickets to an event. The first thing you would say is, "Excuse me! I know you're not talking to me!" They come into the room without saying, "Hi Dad," or "Hi Mom." They begin immediately requesting; how would you respond? Not too happy, I would imagine. And yet, that's how some of us treat our Heavenly Father.

If we decide today that we will change our bad habits of always coming to the Father asking for things and reboot ourselves to spend some time acknowledging and adoring Him, that would be a good start. Be more thankful for what He has done in your life.

Sometimes you don't ask for anything. You spend time worshipping Him and thanking Him for all He's done for you and all the prayers He has answered for you. Thank Him for His unconditional love and mercy

He has extended to you and your family. Reflect on your childhood and how God has kept you and protected you. Think about all the times that He has put his angels around you to keep you from being in a major car accident.

Ponder on all the times He has provided for you and put food on your table. Consider the creation; He provided it all here on earth for us, the moon and the stars, the flowers, and the trees, the hummingbirds and butterflies, the mountains and the valleys, the ocean and the lakes, my God, who can put all of that together? Nobody but My Father! He deserves all the praise!

STEP TWO: <u>We acknowledge who God is and recognize His sovereignty as our Father in our lives.</u> We need to remind ourselves and keep in the forefront of our visual eyesight who God is. (Timothy 1:17 NIV) "Now to the King eternal, immortal, invisible, the only God, be honor and glory for ever and ever." When we find scriptures that remind us of who we are, it refreshes and renews our commitment to Him. And we know that God's word will not return to Him void. (Psalm 62:6-8 NIV) "Truly he is my rock and my salvation; he is my fortress; I will not be shaken. My salvation and my honor depend on God; he is my mighty rock, my refuge. Trust in him at all times, you people; pour out your hearts to him, for God is our refuge." And to remember, we are but chain links in the arena of time fulfilling and completing our purpose in life.

We are alive at this particular time because God ordained it. Psalm 90:1-2 (NIV) "Lord, you have been our dwelling place throughout all generations. Before the mountains were born or you brought forth the whole world, from everlasting to everlasting you are God." Where would we be without His continued faithfulness, His loving kindness, and His unmeasured grace? (Psalm 89:8 NIV) "Who is like you, Lord God Almighty? You, Lord, are mighty, and your faithfulness surrounds you." (Psalm 140:7 NIV) "Sovereign Lord, my strong deliverer, you shield my head in the day of battle."

STEP THREE: <u>Pour out your thanksgiving and praise upon Him.</u> He is worthy of all our praise and glory. Let everything that has breath, praise the Lord. Think about His goodness towards you. Think about how often He has kept you from falling flat on your face. Think about how He healed you from your sickness. Think about how He extends His grace over your life. Think about His provision and how He has miraculously provided for your needs. Think about how He heard your midnight cries and answered your prayers.

Think about how He handled your enemies and made them silent. Think about how you used to be, going to hell before He saved you. Think about His everlasting love that covers you. Think about all the times He has forgiven you and given you another chance. Think about the wisdom He gave you because you asked in a problematic situation.

Think about His sweet Holy Spirit that He so graciously pours out in a time of need to reaffirm that He is with you. Oh My God! What a mighty God we serve. He's good! (Isaiah 25:1 NIV) "Lord. You are my God; I will exalt you and praise your name, for in perfect faithfulness you have done wonderful things, things planned long ago." (Psalm 28:7 NIV) "The Lord is my strength and my shield; my heart trusts in him, and he helps me. My heart leaps for joy, and with my song, I praise him." Psalm (63:3-4 NIV) "Because your love is better than life, my lips will glorify you. I will praise you as long as I live, and in your name, I will lift up my hands."

If we stay in an attitude of gratitude, praise becomes easy, and it's not burdensome because we are thankful for everything. I believe that when we fix our mouths to complain about our circumstances and situations, it is just like Israel in 1 Samuel 8. They were asking for a king. The Lord told Samuel the prophet; it's not you they have rejected, but they have rejected me (The Lord) as their king.

When God allows existing conditions in our lives, and we are the children of God, know this, He has permitted this element in our lives to grow and process us. And God will reveal that to us.

STEP FOUR. <u>We ask God for the forgiveness of our sins.</u> In the Lord's prayer (Matt. 6:9-13), the forgiveness of sins is a two-way street. In other words, it is a continuous flow of the Lord forgiving us, and we forgive others. Incredibly, some of the thought patterns of Christians think that all the forgiveness is on the Lord's side. When in fact, the circle is not complete until we forgive others.

When you hear people say, "I'll never forgive them for what they did to me." Or "I'll never forgive them for what they did to my family." Well, you have just put yourself into a distinctive category and arrangements that will put you in pause mode. Because the word says, "And forgive us our debts, as we also have forgiven our debtors." There is not a gray area, and it is not negotiable! Forgive, and you will be forgiven, period! (Ephesians 4:32 NIV) "Be kind and compassionate to one another, forgiving each other, just as in Christ God forgave you." (Colossians 3:13 NIV) "Bear with each other and forgive one another if any of you has a grievance against someone. Forgive as the Lord forgave you." (Matthew 18:21-22 NIV) Then Peter came to Jesus and asked, "Lord, how many times shall I forgive my brother or sister who sins against me? Up to seven times?" Jesus answered, "I tell you, not seven times, but seventy-seven times." The word of God is crystal clear, forgive!

Sometimes, forgiveness is a process on our part and takes time because the hurt or the offense is so deep-rooted. You feel betrayed and not respected. Or you feel like you were taken advantage of. Only through the precious Holy Spirit can you heal and truly forgive and move on with your life. We take the first step through faith and ask the Lord to help us forgive as the word says. And God honors our obedience.

STEP FIVE. <u>We are petitioning, requesting, and appealing to God for a certain need or desire.</u> A petition is a formal and sometimes written request made to God. And a request is made on behalf of one person. We may be supplicating on behalf of another person because they are not taught in the area of prayer. In a casual interaction with other Christians, the phrase;

"just pray for me." rings out of their mouths in desperation, not knowing what else to do. And the authentic and sincere person of prayer will take that request to God on behalf of another and stand in the gap.

This is really where the spirit of the intercessor comes into play. We can petition and ask on behalf of others. But the difference between asking until we get tired and move on to something else, and asking until we see results, is between a person who prays and an intercessor. An intercessor doesn't stop until they see a manifestation of their prayers being answered.

Many Christians simply don't have because they don't ask. (Luke 11:9-10 NIV) "So I say to you: Ask, and it will be given to you; seek, and you will find; knock, and the door will be opened to you. For everyone who asks receives; the one who seeks finds; and to the one who knocks, the door will be opened." (Ephesians 6:18 NASB) "With all prayer and petition pray at all times in the Spirit, and with this in view, be on the alert with all perseverance and petition for all the saints." (Daniel 9:3 NASB) "So I gave my attention to the Lord God to seek Him by prayer and supplications, with fasting, sackcloth, and ashes." (Philippians 4:6 NASB) "Be anxious for nothing, but in everything by prayer and supplication with thanksgiving let your request be made known to God."

When you have arrived with the mindset of praying for others, not just for you and yours, you have matured to the next level of prayer. Growing in the ministry of prayer also means; you're not taking the credit for answered prayer. You are giving all the glory to God!

STEP SIX. <u>Through the eyes of faith, you are thanking God for hearing and answering your prayers.</u> Your faith in God's word sees the answer. Your faith can visualize and strengthen your position of seeing the answer before it arrives. Your faith will block every fiery dart and every stronghold from the devil and take it captive as the word says, (2 Corinthians 10:4-5 NIV) "The weapons we fight with are not the weapons of the world. On the contrary, they have divine power to demolish strongholds. We demolish arguments and every pretension that sets itself up against the knowledge of God, and we take captive every thought to make it obedient to Christ."

Sometimes you have to get dissatisfied with demonic forces and proclaim loudly, "I see you devil, and I'm not going to take it anymore! I'm tired of you taking advantage of my circumstances. I'm tired of you playing with my emotions. I'm tired of you getting the upper hand! Now Back Up in the Name of Jesus! Thank You, Lord, that you hear my prayers. Thank You, Lord, that the answer is on the way. Thank You, Lord, that You do all things well. Thank You Lord, that all things work together for the good of those who love you and have been called according to your purpose." When you regard your time in prayer over everything else, you are breaking through the railings of inconsistency. With this act alone, you are saying to the devil; "back-up in the name of Jesus. I am no longer deceived; my eyes are wide open.

CHAPTER SEVEN

MAKING A COMMITMENT TO PRAY

With great gratitude and intense appreciation, I praise God for his mercies unto me. I thank God for His faithfulness and consistency in my life. I thank God for every trial, for every adversity, for everything that I thought was inconvenient. I thank God for all the misunderstandings, for all the misinterpreted altercations. I thank God for just loving me in the middle of being myself.

I thank God for His unhesitating and unwavering patience that He has shown me repeatedly. I'm grateful that His hand of mercy overshadows me. As David sat and responded to the Lord; he said, "Who am I, O Lord, and what is my family, that You have brought me this far?" (1 Chronicle 17:16 NIV).

Commitment to pray is simply honoring God with your life. It's not about what people will say or how they respond. It's about obedience. You've heard of the saying, "Obedience is better than sacrifice." God has called all of us to pray! Whether you do it or not is a different story.

I believe the Christian life is about change and transformation and our acceptance of it. We like where we are and don't want to be bothered with change. We are so quick to ask someone to pray for us without imagining that we could pray for ourselves. We wish to cherry-pick out of the word of God what we can and cannot do according to our worldly schedule. Our refusal to grow in the things of God is made by personal choice.

The commitment to pray is a commitment to intimacy with our Father. As you grow in pleasing Him, He begins to change you into His likeness. The things you used to desire are delightfully falling off your agendas of importance. If you are vacillating between the spirit and the flesh; you are not ready to make that first step; remember, the devil will talk you out of this decision every time. But if you are prepared to mature, gird yourself, and keep a watchful eye.

On our first World Mission trip, we went to Port-a-Prince, Haiti. Our schedule was tight, and we had a few days to accomplish and complete our goals. We provided food for an orphanage and a church in need. We wanted to make sure that the funds given to us from the Church, were spent on the essentials. After identifying the needs and concerns, we were told everything was to be purchased in the open market. So, we head out early in the morning the next day to the open market. As we are approaching the Open Market; in my spirit, I am squirming. I know this can't be the Open Market.

Understand when you fly into Haiti, a stench comes in through the vents. That smell is even more pungent in the open market. Okay, the driver parks the van, and the four of us head into this open market. It is sweltering, and sweat is just pouring off me. As we walk through, we are constantly ducking our heads from the artificial plastic ceiling covers, as our feet are dodging potholes of feces and urine. I can't believe my eyes as I see cow meat lying out in the open, on a wood plank, dripping with blood, and it looked like hundreds of flies were on it.

At this point, I am trying to keep a straight face. In the background, you hear Haitians bartering in aggressive arguments over the price of the food. You would think that they are getting ready to fight, but it was told that demeanor was part of who they are. They like to barter before they purchase their food items. All the while, I'm saying, "Lord have mercy, Lord, keep us safe! Lord have mercy." That's all I knew how to pray!

And if that experience wasn't bad enough, it started pouring down rain! We were about a 25-minute walk from the van. When it rains in Port a Prince, the rain is so heavy that you must get to higher ground in a hurry. I'm back to the same prayer; "Lord, have mercy, Lord, keep us safe." The rain waters were up to the middle part of my leg. And all I could think about was the urine and the feces getting on me. Also, my concern was on my leg; somehow, while walking through the market, I scratched my leg from a piece of metal sticking out from a pile of rubble. We managed to get back to the van soaking wet. We had to pause the market shopping until the rain stopped.

At that point, I believed I had to get closer to God. When you're in a foreign land, you have different spiritual climates. Before going to a country, you should do your homework about that nation. I didn't do any of that. And I felt like demons were trying to get me. I knew I couldn't take another trip without learning how to pray from that world Missions trip and pray effectively.

Committing also means you're tired of being tired in prayer. I began crying in my spirit; "Lord, teach me how to pray." I wanted to live a life of unhindered prayer. I desired to be able to pray effectively. I wanted my DNA to have the footprints of prayer. I wanted to be confident in praying and to see my prayers answered. I didn't want to be afraid of praying, but I wanted to be able to leap in my spirit at the opportunity.

The Lord began to teach me as I searched the scriptures. Prayer is not only in my DNA, but it is a passion that engulfs my life. I see everything through the eyes of prayer. You can come to me with any circumstance, and I'm going to see your situation through the eyes of prayer. I believe that in the Christian arena that, we have so many believers who don't pray. It's not even given a second thought. Incredibly, the thing that keeps us close to the Father's heart is the thing we do the least, Pray!

When we decide and commit to pray, we must keep in mind the forces of evil that work overtime to squash our determination to pray. Remember that the promises of God are a process, not a destination. In other words, there are a series of events that come into our lives for the sole purpose of growing and maturing us. The promise we are holding on to brings development, change, and formation. The promises of God shift us closer to the arena of faith, to believe. And in the arena of faith, we are learning to trust God's word to accomplish its purpose.

I believe it was our third trip to New Delhi, India. We were venturing out to a new city named Jabalpur, India. Our host thought it would be good exposure for the Hundredfold Teaching taught by my husband, so we agreed to travel to Jabalpur. The only drawback was that we had to travel by train to get there. They said it took 24 hours to travel by train, so we had to spend the night on the train. We thought we'd get first-class tickets so we could stretch out in the evening to get some rest in our bedroom on the train.

The next day, to be close to the train station for our early morning departure, we had to check into a hotel close to the train depot. Our host didn't want to get caught up in the Delhi traffic for fear of missing our departure time. We both packed light because we planned to travel back to New Delhi in two days.

We rose early the following day to purchase our bedroom train tickets. We secured our tickets and began proceeding down to the sleeper cars. As we walked and passed the train cars, we saw people squatting on the tracks and begging for money. People were everywhere; I could feel the eyes of everyone watching every move we made.

We get to our train car number and climb up the steep steps to get into the train car. I thought I was going to see compartment rooms with doors you could close. Boy, was I ever so wrong! As we walked down this narrow hallway, we saw what looked like bunkbeds, but they were three beds in the open, stacked on top of each other. Directly across this space of bunk beds are three other bunk beds. So, it is six beds in one room, with no door.

You know, I am saying to myself, this can't possibly be first class! Then our host turns to us and says, "Here's your room." I wanted to say, "Stop playing now; take us to our bedroom." The reality of where we are kicks in, and my husband and I give each other a look and suck it up! Okay, the question is asked; "Who's sleeping on the top bunk?" I volunteer to go to the top since I'm the youngest. My husband gets the second bunk right up under me. And the host gets the bottom bunk.

After we identify where everyone is sleeping, the host immediately pulls out this enormous chain, wraps it around his luggage, wraps it around the pole anchoring the bunk beds, and then puts a vast key lock through the chains. He then securely puts his bags under the bed. You know I'm talking to myself, right? What kind of first-class ticket is this that you have to chain your suitcase up like that?" So that was a flashing red light for me. Everything I packed is going up on the top bunk with me!

While we put our stuff on our respective beds, there is a flow of people constantly walking through the hallway, speaking very loudly, selling fragrant Indian food, strong coffee, water, and maps.

At this point in my prayer journey, I have made it a habit always to put aside some time for prayer. And this time is no different. Whatever place or nation we are in, I would look for pillows to put my knees on and a blanket to cover myself up. Then I would grab my CD player and my headphones to play my worship music and be in prayer while my husband was studying. So, while we are on this train, I'm looking for my space.

I climb up to my space on the top bunk because there is no sitting area. Your bed is the sitting area. I get situated on my bed and turn to look straight across from my top bunk bed; an Indian woman is gazing intently at me. The slightest little move I make, her eyes follow. I really want to say. Can I help you? But I refrain from saying anything. I have got to figure this thing out. I dig down in my travel bag and find my travel shawl. Thank You Jesus! I dig further and see some safety pins. Walla! Successfully I secure my private space with two shawls and safety pins. I shared this story because we can always find an excuse to break our commitments.

We can rationalize and justify all our habits, but we just can't find the time to pray. That picture looks fuzzy to me. Our whole existence in this Christian walk is a fellowship and a conversation with our Father. It shouldn't only be in emergency instances that we call on the Lord.

There must be an opening of our eyes, and there must be an awakening, a quickening of our spirits to desire more of God's presence in our lives. Our prayer should be, "Lord, teach me how to break through the barriers of my life so that I may desire more of You. Lord, open my eyes to see the hidden obstacles the devil uses to deceive and derail me. Lord, teach me how to recognize demonic attacks in my life that hinder me from moving forward. Lord, teach me how to break through the difficulties and struggles that put me in a pause cycle. Show me the walls and railings that I have put up against You. Lord, teach me how to pray."

It is my prayer that this book has shed some light on breaking through the barriers on our journey to more intimacy with our Father. It is my prayer for you that your decision has been made to develop a more consistent lifestyle and habit of prayer. Deciding to pray is making a determination and choice toward obedience. You are simply breaking through the barriers of disobedience.

EPILOGUE

If you were like me, I came under strong conviction for my lack of prayerlessness. I was going through the religious motions, but somehow, I felt a deficiency in the area of prayer. Now I know the particular area that needs improvement. You may ask, "What are some of the first steps?" Allow me to share my personal testimony to encourage you to move forward.

In September, in our traditional 11:00 am Sunday morning church service during the congregational hymn, God began to move on the altar of my heart. Everyone was standing on their feet, extending their soprano, alto, baritone, and tenor voices unto God, singing out of the traditional hymnal and all verses of a hymn, of course. You don't attend Church and not sing all four to six verses of a hymn and then end it with a long a-men in unison.

But at that appointed hour one Sunday morning, the precious Holy Spirit was bubbling up inside of me. Much to my surprise, I would join in singing as I always did, in a loud, vibrant alto voice. As I came around the corner of the first verse, this weird language started bursting forth from my mouth, and it wasn't English.

I quickly turned around fearing someone would hear me making this strange noise. So I stopped singing the song but made another attempt about the fourth and final verse of that same song. The same thing happened when I opened my mouth to sing. I finally resolved that the only way I would get through that peculiar hymn was to shut up, so I did.

That Sunday was a day I will never forget. The Holy Spirit was so heavy that I sat with tears rolling down my cheeks, weeping silently throughout the whole service, trying to discreetly wipe away my tears and stay in a composed position.

After Church, different members were coming up to me saying, "are you okay" "is there anything that I could do to help" " you know you can always call me," "it's going to be okay, baby, just hang in there." They had no idea what was going on with me in the spirit. And neither did I at that time. All I knew was that the Holy Spirit was burning on the altar of my heart, and I also knew that the Holy Spirit was reassuring me that "I am with you, be encouraged, don't be afraid, you're on the right track." The scripture that kept coming up in my spirit was "Fear thou not; for I am with thee: be not dismayed; for I am thy God: I will strengthen thee; yea, I will help thee; yea, I will uphold thee with the right hand of my righteousness." (Isaiah 41:10)

We went home after Church as we normally do, ate our Sunday meal, and began to relax. All the while, in my spirit, I couldn't wait to get in my bedroom alone to get in the presence of the Lord. I ensured my husband and our children were well taken care of.

EPILOGUE

Finally, I had time to myself to go before God and finish some unfinished business. I could feel the precious Holy Spirit beckoning me to come aside and spend some time in His presence. I went into my bedroom, and I got down on my knees on the side of the bed, and the Holy Ghost filled and overflowed my cup. And out of my belly (my spiritual belly) came rivers and rivers of living waters from my mouth. (John 7:38) 'He that believeth on me, as the scripture hath said, out of his belly shall flow rivers of living water.'

I began to pray in a heavenly language with tears flooding my eyes and just basking in the presence of the Holy Ghost. It was so beautiful, yet at the same time, it was strange to hear the sound of jabbering coming from my mouth.

After that unforgettable time with the Lord, reality and the devil began talking to me. Reality said, "Oh my God, Oh my God! What have you just done? For crying out loud, you're not a Church of God in Christ, and you don't belong to a Holiness Church; you go to a Baptist Church. What are you doing?" Then the devil said, "what do you think you were doing, nothing but sounding ridiculously stupid." Do you really think the Lord paid attention to that; I don't think so."

It really didn't matter what the devil said at that moment and time because I was full of the word of God that reaffirmed that the infilling of the Holy Ghost is for every believer who believes. (Mark 16:17) And these signs shall follow them that believe; In my name shall they cast out devils; they shall speak with new tongues.

Before that very precious time with the Holy Spirit, the Lord had me searching the scriptures on the Holy Spirit. Remember now, I told the Father I didn't want to be part of a cult, and I wasn't convinced that everyone who believed could speak in tongues. It certainly wasn't practiced in my Church. I was critical of hearing someone speaking in tongues because I said, like everyone else, there must be an interrupter. In my studies, I later learned that the filling of the Holy Spirit is for every believer who desires it.

What are the first steps to take:

1. Decide that you will come out of your comfort zone.

2. Don't be surprised if your friends and family try to talk you out of your desire to be filled with the Holy Spirit.

3. Take it slow. Let the scriptures of being filled marinate in your heart. Get an understanding that having a prayer language is for you.

4. Don't be shocked that every believer will not want to be filled with the Holy Spirit.

5. Schedule a daily time with the Lord where you are praying. Then listen for His response.

6. It is helpful to surround yourself with others that pray in the Spirit. It will help you get stronger and grow in your prayer life.

7. Be ready for the attacks the devil will throw at you to stop you from praying in the Spirit.

8. Set the atmosphere in the place where you are worshipping the Lord. Play worship music that changes your surroundings to a reverential atmosphere.

It is my prayer that anyone who finds themselves reading this book will be filled with the Holy Spirit. It is my prayer that out of their belly will flow rivers of living waters, in Jesus' name. It is my prayer that every barrier is destroyed.

www.ingramcontent.com/pod-product-compliance
Ingram Content Group UK Ltd.
Pitfield, Milton Keynes, MK11 3LW, UK
UKHW022217230426
12048UKWH00016BA/892